Assholes
Win

A short book for your pleasure, amusement and
understanding

CONTENTS

Introduction by Michael Anthony

Chapter 1: It's Your Turn
Chapter 2: Characteristics Assholes Share
Chapter 3: Selfish Nature Required
Chapter 4: The Necessity for Assholes in Business
Chapter 5: The World of Sports
Chapter 6: The Free Pass
Chapter 7: Impact on Dating
Chapter 8: Leadership
Chapter 9: Personality > Mentality
Chapter 10: Situational Awareness
Chapter 11: How to Interact with an Asshole
Chapter 12: Determining Who You Want to Be

About the Author and *The Institute of Human Understanding*

INTRODUCTION

You want to win. You want to get your way. You want your voice to be heard. You want the credit you deserve. You want to be tough and have a backbone. You're tired of being taken for granted, passed over and underappreciated. The question is are you willing to do anything about it.

Sure, you may be tough at times. The word asshole may even be referred. But a true asshole wins at all costs.

They break the rules, do what they want, when they want, disregard others along the way, bulldozing conversations and anything between them and what they want.

They are rewarded too, with promotions, recognition and money, and they see no reason to discontinue this behavior.

If you are not an asshole — full-time, that is — buckle up and see why you aren't getting what you deserve. This book provides a no-nonsense direct analysis with strategies to better understand assholes and influence them, if you're not willing to be one.

Michael Anthony

CHAPTER 1

It's Your Turn

"The world as we have created it is a process of our thinking. It cannot be changed without changing our thinking."

- Albert Einstein

You have been too nice too long. You have likely been taken advantage of. Despite being considerate to others, you have been brushed aside because you don't make a fuss. This is evident in not being given an input on family plans, work projects and everyday common courtesies others enjoy.

It is your turn to let your voice be heard. Let it be known when you don't want pizza for dinner, have no desire to go to Florida on vacation or anything else you're not onboard with. The days of your being disrespected and walked all over are a thing of the past. You can do so in a mild manner, or you can be aggressive and lay out why this is not going to fly any longer. It's your turn to be an asshole.

You already have an asshole side to you. Understand your value and get it. Remember, assholes are everyday people. They have struggles, challenges, self-doubts and are, ultimately, imperfect too. The goal of this book is to help you better understand, succeed with your communications with and use your inner asshole for a better life.

At any stage and in any position in life, you cannot be in charge or lead unless someone is willing to follow. Respect isn't taken, it is given.

Work hard to be a good person but have a backbone. Having an asshole side can in fact help you. Though being an asshole to all, especially to those you perceive to be less than you just because you can, is unnecessary and is detrimental.

Lead by example; show you deserve the opportunity to lead and be an asshole when necessary along the way.

A power struggle may result. Be strategic in your planning and more strategic in your execution. The assholes profiled in this book, didn't get to where they were by going right to the top immediately. They understood it would stop them before they got started. What they did do was to arm themselves with foresight and discipline. They achieved their trajectory to their current success by design. They aligned themselves with winners and were opportunistic, while being prepared.

Some resistance and challenges are sure to arise from others who view you as competition. That is normal.

A power struggle only results when both parties are putting up a fight. An asshole's goal is to be so on point that victory is his by the time the other sides realizes they're in the fight.

We expect leaders to act a certain way. We want confidence, and we want them to believe in what they're saying. We admire those willing to say what they want and do what they want without being scared of the repercussions. Frankly, a small piece of us lives through them. Not everyone has the courage to act in a way that assholes do. Silently, many like their arrogance, confidence, swagger and how they interact. They admire them.

What makes them most admirable is they're winners. Winning, especially in athletics, makes everything OK. People want to be a part of a winning team. Simply put, everyone likes a winner, and assholes win because they don't allow losing to be an option.

The bottom line is: The strongest companies and highest performers have an asshole pushing them to be better and do better. If you want a better future, you'd better hope an asshole is leading you.

Be an asshole today for the betterment of you and those you care about.

CHAPTER 2

Characteristics Assholes Share

"Show me a person without an ego, and I'll show you a loser."

- Donald Trump

Assholes share many of the same characteristics. These characteristics can be both good and bad. In this book you are going to learn how to identify and be one.

It is important to note there's a difference between having an asshole side or moment as opposed to being a total asshole. An asshole is truly bad for themselves and others. We do not condone this type of person.

We do condone being an asshole when it is necessary, as well as understanding how to interact with assholes for the betterment of your life and the lives of those you care about.

Below is a list of bad characteristics assholes share and the good characteristics assholes share:

The Bad

They are **inconsiderate**.

They look out for themselves first. If there is a promotion to receive or credit to be given, they will take it when they may not deserve it. They are ruthless if the situation calls for it. If they want to win at a game, they will do anything within their power to get the circumstances to favor them.

They are **egotistical**.

Over-confidence in certain areas is common. While short-sighted at times, due to their ego taking precedence over big picture thinking, giving is tough for an asshole. They are so confident in their own abilities or beliefs that they will allow it to trump any reasoning or information they potentially receive to save face and protect their ego.

They have a "**me first mentality.**"

They have a "dog eat dog" mentality. If they don't win, they lose. It's as simple as that. They don't view opportunities having a potential win/win outcome. They either win or they lose.

They **lie**.

They will lie to get ahead or prove their point. Most of the time they will justify the lies they tell as necessary or not a lie at all (by creating a gray area). Their internal dialogue can lead to them ultimately believing their lie is the truth with enough convincing and reasoning.

When they are called out on a lie, they don't admit it. Instead, they dig in deeper to save face. This leads to more issues if not in the short term, most definitely in the long term. Almost all lies eventually come to the surface. However, as the quote goes, "If you tell a lie enough times, people will start to take it as the truth, including the liar."

They **lack discipline**.

Discipline is often missing for the gifted or skilled asshole. The reason is they don't need the discipline that may have taken others to achieve the same result. This encourages bad habits. They are often impatient with others who can't produce the results they do. This leads to additional pressure on others and outbursts at inappropriate times.

They are **stubborn**.

They feel their way is almost always the right way. This is taken to the extreme if they have experienced or garnered some success in an area, so they become even more stubborn/adamant about them being right. The reason for this is they have received an affirmation that they are right – it could be the result of a promotion, feedback from others or financial gain. No one wants to give in if they think they are smarter or better than others, especially not an asshole.

They **deflect well**.

Think of a politician. They are asked a direct question and can talk in circles without ever answering the question. The same rings true for the asshole. If they are focused on something, they will direct 100 percent of their focus on that issue or task, deflecting anything else that may come up. They are also very good at deflecting anything brought to their attention that doesn't make them feel good or isn't flattering to them. They don't want to hear anything negative about themselves or their performance, which is when deflecting is most often used.

They **conveniently lack morals.**

In their home life, they may display the perfect life, perfect family and white picket fence. However, they rarely allow morals to get in the way of what they want and when they want it. Cheating, stealing and egotistical fighting are the tip of the iceberg.

They **lack empathy**.

Despite the reasoning on why a project or task did not get performed or performed at a level to their expectation, the asshole does not allow themselves to accept mediocrity or lack of results, regardless of the reason. This can be difficult for some to accept, especially if their reasoning could be something of a personal or significant nature.

They **don't acknowledge being wrong**.

This is viewed as weakness. What is the point of admitting being wrong? It is to show a willingness to do better. When you don't want to reason with others or believe you can do better, there is no benefit, just drawbacks to acknowledge any flaws.

They **don't apologize**.

Apologizing is admitting wrongdoing or room for improvement. They avoid apologizing at all costs. It is only acceptable if management, HR, a board of directors or someone with great influence is pushing it. Apologizing is for losers; it is, in fact, a loss to an asshole. You were wrong — you apologize — you lose. You don't apologize, you don't admit to being wrong; you are never wrong.

They **won't quit.**

Quitting is mental defeat. A negative impact on their reputation often drives their unwillingness to quit. This directly impacts them personally, their family, company and faith in them on decisions they have made, which are clouded in doubt by others, exactly what they don't want (to be questioned). They attribute the success they have up to this point in life to their hard work and willingness to work through difficult times, not allowing quitting to be an option.

The Good

They are **direct.**

They value their time, and they value your time. Despite the short and abrasive approach, their goal is to maximize efficiency. For this reason, they avoid small talk and pleasantries. While offensive to some for being short, they are focused on the reason for their interaction.

They are **focused**.

Since winning is so important to them, they can focus on a task and limit distractions. They hold winning in such high regard that it takes precedence over anything that could distract them. This is an admirable quality and one that garners respect.

They are **results-driven**.

It's all about winning. If you're playing a game to win, you want the best guy to lead your team. Think Michael Jordan. He was an ultra-competitive player considered to be the greatest.

If you're trying to maximize productivity and profit you want the best guy to lead your team. Think Steve Jobs. He would push his team to not stop working until they could state it was the absolute best they could do.

They are **solid leaders**.

If an issue arises, their reaction is always how to fix it and move forward. They do not allow themselves to feel sorry for themselves or what happened, regardless of whether it was fair or not. They are doers. Their accomplishments define their purpose; accomplishments are a result of work and doing.

They **have discipline when it counts**.

Some assholes have discipline and are not naturally skilled or gifted. These are the best leaders. They understand all the important roles others play to make a project, company and family a success. For this reason, they tend to be more effective.

They have been in similar positions to reach their current position, typically by working their way up within the company. This leads to a better understanding of the different facets at play and what may be broken in a certain area or what could be improved.

They are **productive**.

Productivity is more important than being busy. You can be busy, but if you don't have anything to show for it, it's useless. The result determines ultimate productivity.

They are **mentally tough**.

Anyone who has maintained success over time is mentally tough; it is needed to win. It is paramount to succeeding. The daily grind gets exhausting, both physically and mentally. Working long hours and being responsible for the well-being of a business, family or both requires a person who can handle the pressure. This cannot be underestimated.

When things aren't going well, this can send a person over the edge. The mental toughness doesn't stop when a tough situation ends. Mental toughness must have endurance to handle issue after issue and challenge after challenge. When you stay the course and get through each bump along the road, you are more mentally strong than ever before. These experiences allow you to handle difficult situations and challenges throughout life. They are necessary to lead and succeed.

To succeed, the company must prosper at all times to save the company from laying off workers. If the company lays off workers, the domino effect takes hold. Just think, one layoff can drastically impact a family and all those who depend on that person.

Without that job, there is no certainty for food being put on the table, paying for their housing, clothing, medical issues, car payments and much more. This is just the tip of the iceberg of the many things entering a boss' mind.

They have **a clear vision of their goal**.

Despite the numerous distractions that may present themselves, the clear objective to achieve the goal is not lost for winners. This clear vision allows for them to strategize and implement steps to take with the clear purpose of achieving the goal at hand. Any step taken must be one that allows them to get closer to achieving their goal. If it is not clear, it is not likely they'll take it.

They are **physically resilient**.

Your initial thought upon reading "physically resilient" is most likely that of a physically fit or athletic person. However, in this instance it is about endurance, pushing through long hours and tough conditions greater than the normal person can handle.

Sure, it would be easier to get off early or not work nights and weekends when you're sick or preparing for a big trip the following day, but this is not an option. You must push yourself physically and mentally every day to maximize productivity and potential.

Being physically resilient is a form of fitness because your body must handle the extra workload and stress. Many are not prepared for this strain and develop poor health as a result. The most successful are those who can handle the physical demands without having it impact their physical or mental well-being. The good characteristics in assholes lead them to do this with proper exercise, eating habits and stretching/movement throughout the day.

They have an **advantage**.

The advantage an asshole has over the average person is those around them are looking to appease them. Think of the long-time judge Simon Cowell from *American Idol*. The contestants and most viewers may despise him, but any compliment coming from him is held in a much higher regard than the other judges.

People want the asshole to like them.

They are **not considerate.**

This is necessary to achieve results. Leaders that are overly considerate to employees, friends or co-workers rarely get much done. They end up getting too wrapped up in the details that may or may not be to someone else's liking rather than the importance of the actual decision.

Think of a family with parents who ask their kids for input on each decision. This can range from what to eat for breakfast to which movie to watch to which car they drive to the store to what is for dessert that night. It is an absolute recipe for disaster — differing opinions, frustration within the group by those not getting their way, too much weight put on minor decisions causing distractions and tension.

The bottom line is, nice and undisciplined leaders do not generate the results winners want. For this reason, assholes, whether it may be an accurate classification or not by employees and outsiders, are necessary to get the best out of others to ultimately win.

THE THOUGHT PROCESS TO CHANGE

When interacting with a person, specifically an asshole, you will go through the following phases from internal dialogue (thoughts) to external implementation (action). Each of these may appear to be magnified at the time due to the type of person you are interacting with, specifically an asshole.

Hesitation

⬇

Frustration

⬇

Impatience

⬇

Desire = Go for it!

Winners have acknowledged visually identifying a hesitation they've had and go through the imagery and feelings of how it would feel to experience both outcomes of failure and success.

They focus on the feeling success brought them and kept it with them as a reminder of its worth. Self-awareness is the secret of the successful. Being aware of your thoughts and feelings is the only way to control them.

CHAPTER 3

Selfish Nature Required

"You can't be selfish in life without support."

- Unknown

Jimmy Iovine, the music powerhouse who has been involved with the most influential and successful artists in history has let it be known that being selfish is important to succeed. (This is coming from a guy who has worked with John Lennon, Bruce Springsteen, U2, Tupac, Eminem, Lady Gaga and co-founding Beats by Dre with Dr. Dre). You may also know him from his co-founding of Interscope Records, and his role with the '90's powerhouse Death Row Records.

To understand why selfishness is important, we must dig into what it means.

Being selfish is putting yourself ahead of others at all times. If there is something that can further your career or interest, it must take precedence over everything else. This sounds crazy to some, though it is necessary. The focus on achieving success will generate a lot of complaints from others, but it's vital to getting to your desired point to achieve your goals on a mass scale. People will call you names; you'll lose friends, you'll lose contact with others, and people will believe you're an asshole.

If you achieve your goal, it is likely worth it. The reason for this is people gravitate toward those who are successful. It is much easier to support a team that's winning than one that's losing.

To live a life that allows you to be selfish, you must surround yourself with those who either support you 100 percent or are willing to support your dream 100 percent. This is rare to find. This unwavering support is necessary since there will be challenges and temptations to quit along the way. Their support and reassurances can be the difference between reaching your goal or quitting. You never fail; you just quit too soon.

Now, not everyone is striving to be a music executive or pop star, but this message is relevant to your home life, small business life and dreams. Don't be afraid to be selfish. If you are going to be selfish, be committed to being selfish. There is no use in being selfish part-time; part-time won't achieve your goal. You *must* be committed to your selfishness to achieve your goal.

Due to the commitment to selfishness, success is more achievable at a younger age and at a time when you are single. This is because you can take more risk, are not accustomed to a standard of living and do not feel responsible for and to others.

Regardless of your stage of life, without action and a commitment to your goal, by looking out for yourself first, you'll never achieve success.

It is common to hear those at the top of the mountain reflect on countless hours at work, practicing until exhaustion, missing family events, etc. This is typically followed by comments about failed relationships because their significant others were not willing to take a back seat to their careers. It becomes an obsession, which many call a mistress to their relationship.

It is OK to look out for yourself first, as it is unlikely anyone else is going to look out for you before themselves. As long as you achieve your goal and experience success, being an asshole along the way is an afterthought. Everyone likes a winner. All those things missed are typically in the rearview mirror when the view straight ahead is beautiful and promising.

CHAPTER 4

The Necessity for Assholes in Business

"It's when the discomfort strikes that they realize a strong mind is the most powerful weapon of all."

- Chrissie Wellington

The business world is not for the faint of heart. That is why so many successful athletes yearning for the competition find themselves competing in the business world after their careers are over. It's a grind requiring strategic planning, implementation and a dog eat dog mentality.

Typically, the most powerful and wealthy have gotten there by doing whatever it takes, including breaking any rules in their way, lying and cheating. That is the reason why most of these men and women share characteristics such as not being faithful to their wives or husbands and being ruthless when it comes to their money, regardless of who is involved — family, friends, loyal employees, etc.

A real-life business example of this is Steve Jobs.

Steve Jobs co-founded Apple in 1976 with Steve Wozniak and Ronald Wayne. By all accounts, Wozniak was the engineer and design wizard, while Jobs was the driving force for monetizing the company. Ultimately, Apple became one of the most iconic brands in the world and impacted the lives of most. However, this would have never happened without Jobs and his asshole demeanor to run the company.

As he so eloquently stated, "My job is not to be easy on people. My job is to make them better."

He was a world class asshole — tough on workers, cutting out early employees at Apple and denying the paternity of his first daughter for a lengthy period of time.

He did, however, change the world.

From introducing the Mac to the iPhone, iTunes and the iPad, he changed most of our lives. He was a winner, literally disrupting huge niche markets and creating entirely new markets. With the iPhone alone there was no longer a need for a Walkman, alarm clock, video recorder, stopwatch, laptop for internet or emails, a web cam or cameras for world-class photos. He was a visionary.

Respected by most and admired by all, most overlooked his flaws largely because he was successful and ultimately a winner.

In contrast, you may not have known Apple had a third co-founder named Ronald Wayne, and you're not alone. He left Apple due to Steve Jobs being "difficult to work with, stubborn, cold and argumentative." His stock share would be worth more than $35 billion now if he didn't sell out in 1976 for $800.

Assholes are remembered if they're successful. Those who get walked all over, pushed out and left in the dust do not.

From all accounts Wayne was a nice guy. Can you imagine if he was in charge at Apple? Chances are good you wouldn't have heard of Apple or be a part of the world Steve Jobs helped create. Steve Jobs was a fighter, so he pushed Ron Wayne out because he believed he was the correct person to lead Apple.

ANALYSIS OF TRAITS

Macro perspective analysis:

As with all businesses, without profitability, no one has a job. That's the reason why the people at the top are so important to a company's future. They must align themselves with contracts to provide work for their employees to execute. Without the work, there are no jobs. More importantly, without profitability there is no sustainability. You must make money to stay in business, hire more employees and provide pay increases.

Just as people must live within their means to save, purchase big ticket items and get by in life, the leadership of a company must do the same on a much larger level and with much greater pressure.

Micro perspective analysis:

Each worker within a company has an important job to do for everything to work successfully.

As the living legend, New England Patriots Coach Bill Belichick (notorious asshole) has stated, "Everyone knows their job and must do their job."

He has been so strict with these principles that he has released some of the most talented and popular athletes on his teams because they wouldn't consistently do their jobs. These clear expectations have his current roster and future rosters on notice: Do your job, or you won't have a job.

In life everyone also must do their jobs. From entering data into a computer, to mailing out bills, collecting payments, paperwork and so on, these jobs are all important. If one of these jobs isn't performed, it negatively impacts the company as a whole. Don't underestimate the importance of your role.

Why an asshole leader is necessary:

They are fighters.

The only sure way you can lose is by quitting. Assholes don't quit. They understand that and fight for as long as it takes. The only true defeat happens when you give up.

There is a saying I've heard many great athletes use after a game in which their team was on a great run at the end of the game, "We didn't lose, time just ran out too soon." Now how is that for understanding their mental state? Rather than feeling sorry for themselves and labeling themselves as losers since they clearly lost the game, they completely changed their interpretation to a positive tone. This will lead them to future success and momentum. Fighting is necessary to win, as anything worth having isn't given away for free. It requires a fight.

Negotiating contracts and working with clients

The ability to be strong on items of importance in a negotiation is imperative. Regardless of a relationship or friendship, your company's and own interest must take priority.

If the asshole doesn't have the willingness on key issues to acknowledge when their way is wrong, it could lead to major issues. Despite being knowledgeable and right on many items, there will be times in which they're wrong.

The most effective way to have them shift directions is to either a) make it seem as if it is their idea or b) find a way to change directions without any expectation of them admitting they're wrong. While this may seem childish, it is effective and comparable to marriage. If you're married, you already know.

Clients want confidence in those they work with. They ultimately must believe in you, and your confidence gives them reassurance. Your confidence combined with superior results/service leads to a premium you can charge.

Holding third parties accountable

Not fearing confrontation and being in a powerful position, the asshole can hold third parties accountable for overcharging or providing services below expectations or not performing. If they don't project this authority, there are cost overruns, compromised quality of service and reduced production, and the company will continually be taken advantage of. Not so with an asshole who is on their A game.

Holding employees accountable

Steve Jobs said it best, "Some people aren't used to an environment where excellence is expected."

Employees have a job to do. They have skills or training provided to do their job. If one person does not perform the job or performs it at a substandard level, the supervisor must address it immediately. If it is not addressed, the employee will continually allow their efficiency and quality of work to decrease because they see it as acceptable. This can affect the whole immediate team and, ultimately, the company.

This is common in a set up where some workers slack off. Once a worker gets away with forming bad habits, which directly impacts the efficiency and quality of work produced, others take notice and tend to allow their level of productivity and quality of work to decrease as well.

That is why an asshole must be there to hold them accountable. The last thing an employee wants is to be surrounded by mediocrity.

Pushing employees to be the best they can be.

When excellence is expected, employees excel and feed off one another. This is not done by letting them have complete freedom to come and go as they please, distract themselves with their cellphones and take longer lunch breaks than permitted.

Assholes expect and push for structure. Structure increases productivity. Some workers can't handle it. That's OK. If you can handle it, you are likely to be rewarded.

Despite the outside perception the asshole likes to give back and wants to be liked. If you make the asshole look good, you will be rewarded.

Promotions, raises, bonuses and satisfaction with your job all play hand in hand, which is not possible without an asshole. In all likelihood the asshole will show their softer side and joy in giving those bonuses.

Insight — asshole rationale

The rationale is assholes have high expectations of themselves, and they also hold others in high regard. Many fail to understand that someone only will have high expectations of you if they believe in you. Many workers will view this type of boss as an asshole boss, until they see what this boss could push them to do. Winning and success as the result cures everything.

But you don't need the money!

Money isn't necessarily the driving factor for the wealthy asshole. It is simply a way to keep score. You may know people who don't need the money yet continue to work, buy and sell items or invest. This becomes a challenge for them to stay sharp, especially as they age.

Once someone masters a business or game, it becomes even harder to leave. Just think of how many athletes have trouble retiring. It is much easier to quit a game when you aren't good or quit a job that you dislike.

Jeffrey Pfeffer, Professor of Organization Behavior at Stanford wrote in his article in the *Journal of Management Studies*, "Why the Assholes are Winning: Money Trumps All," "Instead, numerous behaviors suggest that it seemingly doesn't matter what an individual or a company does, to human beings or the environment, as long as they are sufficiently rich and successful. Money, indeed, trumps all. Moreover, because money can serve as a signal of competence and worth, no amount of money is ever enough. Much like a drug, money and status become addictive."

If you're winning, have lots of money and succeed, most people will overlook your being an asshole.

CHAPTER 5

The World of Sports

"The worse things are, the better I am."

- *NBA Hall of Famer Jerry West*

Commitment and persistence are the two key qualities of winners. Winners share a greater commitment to achieving a desired result, and their persistence changes their "luck," where others may give up due to difficulty or bumps in the road. In the end, we all become what we overcome.

They are also well-aware of the potential pitfalls and distractions that can have a negative effect on them from achieving their goals. For this reason, they are self-aware in addition to being extremely focused on the goal at hand.

Examples of this include the language they use and refrain from using.

"TRY"

The word "try" doesn't register for most winners. It doesn't enter into their vocabulary. They don't believe in *trying* their best. They believe in *doing* their best. They expect the same out of others. Try is an attempt; doing is a commitment. Show you are committed to them, and they will take notice.

"BUT"

The word "but" negates the previous thought(s) or statement(s) made. When communicating with an asshole, they expect direct concise talk. Inserting "but" into the conversation clearly states you are adding more to the conversation than they need or desire.

For instance, "We had a great turn out and raised a lot of money, *but* we fell short of our goal by $50." The bottom line is: You fell short of the goal by $50. The previous statement and inserting *but* added more words and took more time than necessary. Know your audience, if it is an asshole, be direct. An asshole is not looking for sugarcoating by beating around the bush; be direct and move on. It will serve you well. If they want more details, they will ask.

In sports, simply put, there is a winner and a loser. The asshole winner's desire to win produces unbelievable results, a never-quit attitude and a mentality of winning by all means necessary.

"FEEL"

Very few coaches and players care about how you feel. They do care about how you want to feel. The ultimate goal for everyone is to feel great. A great feeling comes from visible improvement, success and victory.

The winners visually identify a hesitation they may have had and visualize how it would feel to hesitate and lose. Rather than experiencing the loss first-hand, their simulation of it keeps them clear of hesitating in the future. In doing so, they can remain focused on what is right, moving toward it without hesitation and feel good about it.

Winners choose to focus on the feeling success brought them. As a result, they take the steps most likely to garner the best "feelings," i.e. outcomes.

Baseball Legend Pete Rose

Big Red Machine fans and blue-collar workers alike love Major League Baseball's all-time hit king Pete Rose.

Playing for 24 years, being a 17-time All-Star, having the most hits in MLB history among many other records for a guy who made the team by try-out as a long shot is truly the American Dream.

His nickname was "Charlie Hustle" for his hard work.

While many love Pete, others feel as if he never knew how to not go 100 percent or take it easy. This was on full display in the 1970 All-Star game.

The night before the game Pete and his wife had dinner with friends, who just so happened to be the opposing team's catcher and his wife.

During a tight game a play was made at the plate and Pete Rose was running toward home to score the potential game-winning run. The only thing between him and the plate was the catcher. He bulldozed his friend, the catcher, whom he had dinner with the night before and scored the game-winning run.

Pete wanted to win, and the catcher was blocking his way to score to help win. Pete would do anything to win. Some may consider this an asshole move.

Pete Rose's team won the game. Do you know the catcher's name?

Neither do I.

You do remember the winner's name, though, Pete Rose "Charlie Hustle," all-time hit leader, winner.

CHAPTER 6

The Free Pass

"A body of men holding themselves accountable to nobody ought not to be trusted by anybody."

- *Thomas Paine*

Celebrities have become so engrained in our society, many people feel as if they know them on a personal level. Having paparazzi reporting any update in their lives and our reality TV-obsessed society may have something to do with it. So, what better way for us to demonstrate the double standard winners benefit from in life. They get a free pass.

Any normal person would be ridiculed and exiled from family, friends and work groups for some of the actions they have been involved in.

By dissecting theses celebrities on a macro level and targeting past specific actions, my goal is for you to understand how they have been able to use their asshole actions and/or general approach of "me first" to their benefit to win and excel in life. Winning, then, comes full circle to make these shortcomings and past actions acceptable or overlooked. So, not only did they use asshole moves to get ahead, they benefit from these same asshole moves to stay on top.

Note any normal person can't get away with this. Assholes that achieve great success are given many free passes. This is seen on a regular basis. Think of a great athlete or a business executive, both considered elite due to the results they produce. If they act out or do something that is viewed in an unfavorable manner, they are given a little slap on the wrist if any discipline at all. In contrast, the no-name player or lower level employee is fired on the spot or disciplined harshly. No one said it was fair. It is reality.
One label synonymous with the term asshole is the playboy. Women and men alike publicly use the term in a less than flattering manner. Many men will publicly express dismay but privately admire them or

aspire to be them. One person who is linked with the term playboy is Hugh Hefner, both as a person and as a brand.

HUGH HEFNER

There are some exceptions to the rule, such as Hugh Hefner of *Playboy*. Hefner appealed to the mainstream and most men admired him and many women viewed him favorably. Sure, some may view him as a creepy old man dating young women, but most brush it off.

By all accounts a man who does not want to commit to a woman, sleeps around and is selfish in his lifestyle is considered an asshole. Hefner avoided the label. He made no apologies for his lifestyle. He divorced his first wife in 1959, just six years after launching *Playboy* to focus on *Playboy*. He dedicated his life to *Playboy*. This is viewed as a true asshole move, selfish and self-serving.

The media loved him. Men looked up to this man approaching 90 with multiple girlfriends, all young enough to be his granddaughter (disturbing to see in writing, isn't it?). He was wealthy, powerful and got many free passes.

He published nude photos without the permission of many celebrities including, Madonna, Vanna White and the most famous cover-girl of all time, Marilyn Monroe. Talk about feeling violated as a woman. This would not fly today.

After his death, it became more well-known about his curfews for girlfriends, monetary allowances and previous articles were again brought to light detailing his attempts in the earlier days of *Playboy* to normalize the sexualization of underage girls.

Two underaged childhood stars were featured in *Playboy*, Brooke Shields and Eva Ionesco. Eva ended up suing her mother, but the clear damage to her for the rest of her life had been done.

It is as if, Hefner was grandfathered in to have a permanent free pass. His achievements and reputation exceeded his actions. He became a living icon, who is now a dead icon. Masterful branding led to winning; winning is all that most remember.

SHAWN "JAY-Z" CARTER

It is common knowledge Carter started in the Marcy housing projects in Brooklyn, New York. He raps about it in his songs and acknowledges dealing drugs in his teenage years. He has boasted with pride in detailing having enough cash to buy a Mercedes before he could get his license.

Many kids look up to him and follow his steps. Adults take his lyrics with a grain of salt because they like his music. However, why has no one asked how many people died and families were destroyed as a result? The answer: No one cares to ask, kids look up to him, adults like his beats, and he is living a better life as a result.

He is one of many musicians who objectify women, call them demeaning names, refer to illegal activities, and are all viewed as role models for the youth and widely accepted in pop culture today.

Listen to the lyrics of the song "Big Pimpin'." Why did the "me too" movement not pursue his past actions or being in the presence of an underage Aalyiah with R. Kelly when she was 14 years old?

Substance takes a back seat in today's world of entertainment. As many of you know, getting the story out first is more important than getting it right. By the time a correction is made, the opinion has already been formed.

Jay-Z is now known as a mogul – the first hip hop billionaire. His label is synonymous with how people perceive him, not noticing or acknowledging his asshole moves along the way to get there.

ARNOLD SCHWARZENEGGER

If there is anyone who has lived a full life and deserves to be admired, it's Arnold Schwarzenegger. Born in Austria to a lower to middle class family, he followed his dream of bodybuilding to unparalleled heights.

He put bodybuilding on the map. He won a record seven Mr. Olympias and Mr. Universe four times (one time as an amateur), was International Powerlifting Champion, served in the military in his native country of Austria, came to America, became a millionaire prior to Hollywood success at the age of 30, a famous model, one of the highest paid movie stars of all-time, married a Kennedy, founded the Arnold Classic (World's Largest Multi-Sport Festival now on six continents) and was the governor of California.

Not bad for a man with a heavy accent most would be self-conscious about and no family connections to give him an advantage in accomplishing one, let alone all these huge feats.

In the legendary film *Pumping Iron* Arnold reflects on the death of his father. While most would immediately find a way to return home upon hearing the news by a phone call from his mother to console her, Arnold didn't.

He was two months out from a competition and used the rationale that he couldn't bring him back or do anything about it, so there was no point. In watching him discuss this time in his life, it was as if he brushed it off as a distraction, he could not welcome due to his laser focus on the upcoming competition. (He won.)

Many would state this to be selfish, inconsiderate and an asshole move. I wouldn't disagree with you. However, Arnold hasn't achieved the success he has achieved by allowing himself to get distracted from any goal he had within his sights.

JOHN F. KENNEDY

The 35th President of The United States of America's father was said to have made the family money during Prohibition by bringing into the country banned alcohol and engaged in backroom politics with his sons to further John Kennedy's career.

Plus, he was a notorious philanderer, friends with Frank Sinatra and on the receiving end of Marilyn Monroe's infamous "Happy Birthday, Mr. President" song in which she leaned over with her cleavage out (in front of his wife Jackie Kennedy).

He was young, handsome, well-spoken and powerful. He had luxuries the average person couldn't dream of having. From living a privileged life in New York City, to summering on the ocean in Hyannis Port,

Massachusetts, boating to Martha's Vineyard and marrying debutante Jacqueline Bouvier, he was living the American dream.

However, like most assholes it's never enough.

Despite having the American dream and being elected one of the youngest presidents in United States history, he couldn't be content with his beautiful life and wife. He was known to have many women in and out of the White House, most notoriously reportedly Monroe.

Most of the things he did that would be considered asshole moves were long in the closet. Let's just say if he was around today with smart phones and 24-hour scandal-craving news sites, he'd be remembered much differently.

After his assassination at age 46, he has been memorialized more than any president since Abraham Lincoln. Today, he is memorialized with airports, roads, museums and more being named after him. He's had numerous books written about him, his face on our currency and as a style icon. Assholes win.

YOU

Despite not being a celebrity, you can get a free pass when you produce. The result is greater than the collateral damage of feelings and ethics, when the result is great enough.

The bottom line is you're an asshole too. At times, we all are. It may not always be intentional, but, as you know, you can't please everyone.

To succeed personally or professionally, you must allocate time for yourself. Rest assured, someone will not be happy with you prioritizing what is best for you over their demands or expectations.

Being intentional with your use of time is equally as important as what you do with your time.

CHAPTER 7

Impact on Dating

"However successful you are, there is no substitute for a close relationship. We all need them."

- Francesca Annis

Assholes date like the rest of the world. These highlights and insights are intended to provide clues on identifying an asshole and learning how to understand them. Through identification and understanding, you can then use tips within this book to manage them and your interaction with them better. You can also learn when it is beneficial to be an asshole yourself.

Below are some characteristics you may find:

- They tend to act better than you.

It could be privilege, wealth, business success, accomplishments or affirmations, but they believe they have a lot more to offer someone than they have to receive. This is evident in the way they may talk to you or others and their level of expectations – from service at a restaurant to food to finer things in life.

- They just want sex or are unwilling to wait.

Remember, they are used to getting what they want. While material items can be purchased and they can have their workers do what they want when they want it, sex is a different story. Sex is not something they can expect or get on demand. It is one of the few things not within their control, which can lead to frustration for someone who is used to controlling most aspects of their life.

- Charm

Charm is a tool that can be used most effectively. The asshole understands the power being charming can have to get ahead in life to get what they want.

It cannot be understated; charm is one of the easiest things to turn on, while being one of the quickest to turn off as well. If an asshole doesn't get what they want quickly after turning on the charm, true colors show, and the charm immediately is turned off.

- Arrogance

They believe they should be treated better. They expect to sit immediately or shortly after arriving at a restaurant, have high standards for service and little tolerance for incompetence. This is viewed as being an asshole. However, they hold themselves to the same high standard.

- Power struggle

They're used to being the person in charge and having the final say. It is not uncommon for them to not want to give up control at all. This includes minor items such as choosing a place to eat for dinner to larger and more important items.

- Consideration, lack there of

They care about themselves first and foremost. This has served them well throughout business and life. It's not that they don't care about you or your feelings, it just doesn't enter their minds.

- What they want

For someone who is used to getting their way, they gravitate toward wanting the most desirable items. Of course, the most desirable item(s) happen to be what they can't have. They will undeniably want those who pay them the least attention, what is perceived to be hard to get and the ultimate "prize."

- Cheating

Remember, they are concerned with their needs and wants, first and foremost. With their needs and wants placed above their significant other along with anyone they may meet or hookup with along the way, they proceed without any consideration on how it may impact others. This could be a fling or could be ongoing behavior. One thing is for certain; they don't care until they hit rock bottom, which would require drastic changes to their lifestyle and an emotional awakening, which is unlikely for most true assholes.

CHAPTER 8

Leadership

"The challenge of leadership is to be strong, but not rude; be kind, but not weak; be bold, but not a bully; be thoughtful, but not lazy; be humble, but not timid; be proud, but not arrogant; have humor, but without folly."

- Jim Rohn

Those that go the safe route rarely experience great success. Most accept this and are satisfied with the safe route. Assholes are not.

Very few people have the courage to think outside the box and challenge the norm. Most people prefer to go with a "safe job," due to their perceived view of stability of the large employer or anything that is viewed as less risky in any aspect of life.

There is a role for those playing it safe; they're followers. Leaders cannot lead without followers. The majority of people look to follow rather than lead. For this reason, there is great opportunity and less competition to be a leader.

There are many characteristics and skills that are necessary to be a good leader, however, the most important is action. Followers are hesitant and therefore do not act for one reason or another. It may be concern about what others may think, the possibility of failure or lack of confidence flanked by self-doubt. For these reasons, an asshole personality is necessary and often proves to be the perfect leader.

They are self-confident, are willing to ruffle feathers by challenging the norm, take chances that may involve high risk and ultimately high reward. Furthermore, their egos can allow them to ignore the potential pitfalls due to their utmost focus on achieving the result they desire.

This is necessary for an effective leader. Someone who can create a vision and culture in which others can follow. People want to be a part of a team. Correction, people want to be a part of a *winning* team.

Leaders think differently.

The best example to display this are the two types of reframing detailed within Neuro-Linguistic Programming.

1) Content — details

2) Context — events

The asshole may not be familiar with the terms, though they tend to be masters at reframing. They will view the content differently from the masses, which is necessary because if everyone viewed content the same and thought the same, there's little to no innovation or improvement.

They also view context differently. This is more of a big-picture approach. The head of a company must be a big-picture thinker to inspire others and lead the company to growth.

Content — details example:

Having an expensive bottle of wine next to a plastic cup would make most think the cup must be of superior quality. However, the asshole would be more apt to see the cup as being cheap and plastic due to noticeable scratches that appear on plastic but wouldn't appear on glass. Going against the grain is common among the leaders in the world today. Almost everyone becomes a lazy thinker. Those who achieve great success, make breakthroughs and change the world understand that thinking differently is a necessity.

Context — events example:

Upon hearing news of bombing a foreign country, many felt outraged because bombing can only lead to more death. The asshole would dig further to find out more of the details to understand the context better. In doing so, they may determine the bombing was justified as it was done on a drug compound in which a rescue mission of hostages was already complete, and they wanted to destroy the infrastructure of the cartel.

Leaders thinking differently are necessary. If not, everyone involved will be in trouble. This is important for negotiating, handling disagreements and, ultimately, achieving goals.

Most assholes are strong **negotiators.** They negotiate from a position of strength. They only want to negotiate a deal in which they view as beneficial to them personally or the company. This is important. At a time when others are concerned with keeping friendships, relationships and business dealings on cordial terms, the asshole cares about profitability and the company's future.

Why is this attitude important to you? That job security you hold dear to your heart, pay raises and future promotions hinge on it.

Most assholes are also **argumentative**. They like to question why a leader within the company is doing a project or task a certain way. The expectation is to hear a reason that makes sense. If it does not, they will hold all parties accountable. They expect the best in terms of ideas and execution. Remember, your and their future hinges on it.

This can get sticky, as many may become offended or embarrassed when questioned in public. However, this is not a time to get emotional, it is a time to show why you are a great asset who does great work.

If you cannot, you may receive a reprimand, a public shaming and silent treatment moving forward. These are signs of disappointment and frustration. Despite being down about this result, you must work harder to eliminate this from happening again and be prepared for next time since there is always a next time. Once that next time comes, it will be even more impactful if you are on your A game.

Most assholes will take credit from others and **do anything to get ahead.** It's a common joke in the business world that assholes listen to the radio station *WIIFM* – What's In It For Me.

Everything they do has the thought "what's in it for me" at the front of their minds. Despite giving the appearance of caring about others or the company, they are continually thinking of how it will impact them — good and bad. This leads to calculated decisions to maximize their good and exposure on everything from ideas to volunteer work, despite minimum involvement. They are quick to publicize and take credit for what they have little to no involvement in. It's all about making themselves look better to get ahead.

Most assholes are **focused on goals**. Just as a company's stock must meet or beat expectations for it not to go down, leaders must continually push forward to be better than they were the day before. Improvements in productivity and results are necessary.

The most successful leaders know their numbers. They base their goals on numbers, not feelings. You can measure numbers on a daily, weekly, bi-weekly, quarterly and yearly basis. You can bet your boss or the head of a company knows exactly where the business stands year over year, last year versus this year. Numbers are even measured comparing previous years. The reason why this is so important is to get an accurate pulse of the company's health, where opportunities may be within the company and where areas are falling behind.

Ultimately, the more focused on goals the leader is the better he understands the business. This may lead to high expectations, pushing their workers hard and creating a more intense work culture. The best leaders apply pressure to themselves and hold themselves to a high standard. Having a leader who does this often leads the company to excel and prosper in most business climates. A good leader is invaluable and often enough is an asshole.

CHAPTER 9

Personality > Mentality

"Obstacles are what you see when you take your eyes off the goal."

- *Legendary football coach Vince Lombardi*

Assholes are typically **impatient**. They see no reason to wait until a later date when they could positively impact results immediately.

Their focus is on **results**. Impatience can be a curse if implementation is delayed or out of reach. Impatience but can also be an asset when channeled correctly because it can lead to extraordinary results, whether it be a revolutionary product, improvement or productivity.

Assholes ultimately want to be **respected**, being liked is an added bonus or curse. They have a tough shell because they understand their role is not to be everyone's friend but to be the rock others look to, while holding everyone to a standard. It may be to produce at work, keep the family's home life stable or keeping others in check so everyone is doing the best they can for themselves and for others.

Assholes want to be viewed as **tough** and act accordingly. Being viewed as tough is a badge of honor for an asshole. They see this as an affirmation that their persona mirrors what they believe to be necessary to be effective.

Assholes are **focused**. Correction, **winners are focused**. If you have ever heard an athlete describe how they felt in a period of success in a sport, it gives you direct insight into their mental state in that moment. For instance, a basketball player may state they were "in the zone" after making 10 shots in a row or a golfer may state the hole seemed "huge" as getting the ball in the hole became much easier.

Their mental state gives them further confidence based on their momentum as a result on their supreme focus to have repetitive successes.

In the business world it could be the feeling that "everything is going right" when they are having success with each client or potential client they speak to in a day. Equally important to focusing on the positive is focusing on the details necessary to achieve the result they hope to achieve.

Assholes **are comfortable in discomfort.** Many leaders believe the time to shine is not in times of ease but in times of difficulty. Weightlifters attribute joy to the burning sensation they get after numerous repetitions, while the normal person stops and focuses on the discomfort. The weightlifter not only has a positive belief associated with it, but truly sees this as the time in which the real workout starts and the muscle grows. In this moment they are focusing on the joy from the muscles contracting and feeling the fibers stretch. Now that is focus!

Assholes don't believe in ties, only **winning**. They either win or lose. Rarely will you hear them acknowledge such thing as a "moral victory"; they do not allow that sort of thinking to enter their minds.

This is important for others to understand. One must not attempt to cheer up an asshole after a loss, but rather move on in the same manner they would – disappointment, regroup and action!

Thus far, you may have only thought of an asshole in a role of a boss or executive within a company. I want to do a paradigm shift in how you are thinking.

Think of a coach or a parent that is tough. In fact, it may have been a coach or parent whom you respect more now than you ever did then. You may not have liked them at times or their approach, although you clearly understood their expectations.

Understanding expectations is the only way to consistently meet or exceed expectations.

Furthermore, many of the expectations could be as simple as being on time or being held responsible for your actions. Assholes get stuff done, and their expectations often yield superior results from those who may need the structure they demand.

That coach who made you run when you showed up to practice late or quit on a play was instilling the necessary work ethic and discipline required to survive and excel in life. You show up to your job on time and don't quit on yourself. The same rings true for the parent who is tough on their kid, requires them to help around the house and get a job.

There is no wonder why the most successful coaches are ex-military men – Coach K at Duke, Coach Belichick with the New England Patriots and legendary basketball coach Bobby Knight. They all have expectations that any onlooker can see, discipline within their teams, which have yielded great results – winning.

In a family setting, the parent(s) who helped instill the work ethic by not giving you whatever you wanted growing up, as an adult is the parent you are eternally grateful for since it prepared you for life. As a parent myself, I can attest to wanting to protect your kid and doing everything possible to ensure they have a better life than you.

However, struggles and challenges are good for building character. Working through the struggles and challenges is great practice for them because they are sure to experience these throughout life. This is more common in a two-parent household where one can have the "asshole role."

In contrast, a single parent household (in particular the fatherless households), lack the structure and discipline that is beneficial later in life. This is not to say there are not fantastic mothers, who are amazing parents who keep their kids in line, but the missing father figure hurts most households. When the structure and discipline is lacking, the kid will appear happy. Who wouldn't be happy being able to do whatever they want.

However, this is not beneficial for their future. As they get older, they can't do or get whatever they want. This sets up massive disappointment, lack of coping skills and can lead to suffering as an adult, which could be lessened if they understood these principles as a kid.

Ultimately, their future suffers and that directly impacts their quality of life, future family and career. Assholes are necessary.

Structure > Discipline > Growth

Foundation > Future Success

Truth

CHAPTER 10

Situational Awareness

"The ultimate value of life depends upon awareness and the power of contemplation rather than upon mere survival."

- Aristotle

The most effective assholes learn to not always come across as an asshole. They can filter their comments and actions in limited interactions. For instance, they may treat their mother or the head of a valuable client account in a much more polite, patient and endearing manner.

When interacting with an asshole, the true opportunity in getting what you want covertly is not by being overly aggressive but by being more aware of how to communicate. Building rapport is a great place to start.

ESTABLISHING RAPPORT

Rapport is a close and harmonious relationship in which the people or groups concerned understand each other's feelings or ideas and communicate well.

Establishing good rapport with anyone is important. It can lead to stronger relationships with family members, friends and a better camaraderie at work.

What many fail to remember is that good rapport is more than just asking questions. While it may be good to learn by asking questions, you don't want to come across as an interrogator. Truly interact with them by injecting an experience that confirms their opinion. This will create positive momentum and further the conversation. Repeat what they state and nod your head, showing you are digesting the information and agreeing. Sharing information is also important since it shows trust and helps form or strengthen a relationship.

It is important not to go on a five-minute story to their one-minute answer; the goal is still to allow them to talk more than you. A simple head nod and making eye contact are also great tools to show you are digesting their information and paying attention. It can also be construed as agreeing with them, which doesn't hurt.

In contrast, communicating aggressively or at a time when their guard is already up will yield asshole responses, a lack of listening and frustration.

However, if you catch them at a time when their guard is down and you approach them covertly, you should receive more receptiveness to ideas, opinions and whatever your goal may be. Just be certain to be on your A game. Know your questions, reasoning for the discussion with him and what your goal is. If not, the asshole will rear his head and eat you alive.

If an asshole treats you well, you will have your opportunity to return the favor. If they go out of your way to treat you poorly, you will most likely have your opportunity to return the favor.

The most successful assholes know their audience.

MONEY, POWER, CRISIS

Power and money are said to either change people or show off who they really are. With assholes, this is no different.

How you treat others is the most visible characteristic. Those looking to get ahead professionally and personally far too often look past the person equal and below them on the business or social ladder. What they fail to realize is that many of those above them on the business and social ladder are observing how they treat those they view as beneath them.

The more money and power someone has the more they are likely to talk down to others, treat them as beneath them and be inconsiderate. Far too often, they are disconnected from a world they once knew — normalcy and decency.

Real leadership is being able to interact with the CEO down to the janitor working nights, without appearing out of place.

Having power and money provides many benefits that those who have neither could ever fathom. They are given additional leeway, the benefit of the doubt and more credit for success than they may deserve. Money and power go hand in hand.

Crisis is an opportunity. It is an opportunity to lead, show your value and earn your keep. This is common. Think of the last time the country was truly united, regardless of politics. Most would agree on 9/11. The crisis brought the nation together.

Crisis can also show who is unwilling to follow or support leadership. Your awareness of those who are supporting, resisting and indifferent is necessary to successfully lead a family, a company or team.

UNDERSTANDING A LOSE/LOSE SITUATION

Some assholes are lost causes. They have a great attention for situational awareness and position themselves appropriately. Despite the temptation and attraction, we all seem to have the want to "help" others and try to "change" them. This is an exhausting position to be put in and should be avoided at all costs. The assholes that are lost causes will pounce on an opportunity to use you and benefit like a shark acts on blood in the water.

They will appear grateful and open for your help but rarely offer or insist on returning any of your good deeds by good deeds of their own.

They will take advantage of your good intentions. They will use your time, welcome your generosity and collect to the fullest for their benefit. They may show a flash of decency or appreciation, which provides you hope there is a nice person under all the bad you are attempting to see through. Remember, the true lost-cause assholes are master manipulators and get what they want.

Unfortunately, they don't know any better. They revert to what they know — me first. This is a difficult acknowledgment for someone to reach because we tend to look for the best in people.

A small percentage of people are true lost causes. By the time everyone discovers they're lost causes, it's probably too late. You have invested a lot of time, energy and effort. It is unfortunate.

This is discovered at three potential times:

1) Upon meeting someone, and you avoid them altogether. As a result, you are never putting yourself in the position to be potentially hurt or taken advantage of.

2) A major life event takes place, and the true colors of this lost cause show. This is likely to involve someone you expected them to hold in high regard, although their actions show a person disengaged from the person and situation.

3) Once you are outside the bubble, you can see from afar what was too difficult to accept from within. Sometimes this happens when time apart allows you to look at the lost cause, past situations and your relationship with them more clearly or after death. Once they die, it becomes crystal clear, similar to when someone gets out of a bad relationship. You don't realize how bad it is or was until you are out of the bubble.

CHAPTER 11

How to Interact with an Asshole

"You're an asshole, you know that, Haller?"
I nodded and headed back to the door.
"When I need to be."

- Michael Connelly, The Gods of Guilt

So, how do you handle, interact and succeed with an asshole? Take these tips into consideration when dealing with an asshole or someone who is in an asshole mood. These will serve you well.
First, don't push your beliefs on an asshole. They think they know more than you, so why would they want to acknowledge your knowing something they don't? Despite your being right or having a superior idea, they will not be open to it unless they can take credit for it or benefit from it in some way.

When an asshole calls you for something, be ready. Don't waste any time; they view time as the most important item anyone has, and it's not infinite. Being considerate of their time is mutually beneficial to your time.

Offer value immediately by showcasing what you have to offer or what you are presenting in a way that benefits them. By showing value, you're demonstrating your value and effectiveness and building trust for the future.

If you do not perform, you must acknowledge it to them. State directly it will not happen again and work your hardest to assure it doesn't happen again. To take it a step further, you must be extra prepared moving forward to make it up. You can be certain you will have a chance again. You can either *wow* the asshole or lose any respect, role or hope they had for you.

Showing you can be relied on is as important as anything to an asshole. Being reliable shows stability and yields trust. Progress is important in every aspect, as an asshole believes you are moving forward in the right way or backwards in the wrong direction. They want to count on a select few to form a team as their inner circle, in their career and in their circle of friends.

When interacting with an asshole, you must be self-aware. This is especially important in acknowledging they want to be the one in charge. While this may frustrate some, it does not frustrate those who put it into context. Just think of parenting up to your parents. Have you not had to show your parents a different way of thinking without talking down to them or making them feel dumb? Exactly.

Stroke their ego by outsmarting them. Feed their need for appreciation and respect by complimenting them. Using a sandwich approach is very effective. The sandwich approach puts a suggestion/opportunity for changing how they do things in between one or two items in which you compliment them on how well it works, or they do it.

The sandwich approach works, as most people are defensive with any criticism, suggestion they could be doing better and open up more once they put their guard down. Their guard comes down quickly with flattery.

The most important thing to keep in mind when interacting with an asshole is to simply pick and choose your battles, while keeping your eye on the prize. Whether you are wanting to develop a friendship, respect, trust or a business relationship, the asshole will rub you the wrong way, state things that are not nice and may be harsh.

However, if you were to challenge each thing you didn't like or had an issue with, you both would be miserable and at each other's throats. If you keep your eye on the prize and focus only of items of paramount importance to you, you should fare much better.

One additional piece of advice is to pick and choose your battles around the items you can win. You don't want to take an asshole head-on regarding one of the most important issues to them. Identify the issues where you have a shot to win and focus on those.

GETTING PEOPLE TO CHANGE

Questioning one's beliefs is the most powerful and effective way for change to take place.

The 13 Steps for Getting People to Change Process:

1. Understand their perspective.

2. Identify holes in their perspective. Ask questions in a non-combative way (indirectly pointing out holes).

3. Let them digest the questions to answer.

4. Listen to their answers attentively.

5. Give an example of something similar you experienced (showing it's OK to change their beliefs).

6. Let them respond.

7. Give brief feedback responses, such as "OK," "interesting." (Don't push too hard, just listen and nod your head.)

8. Let them continue on after your brief feedback.

9. Ask questions referencing additional holes with their perspective.

10. Cite examples to bring the holes out more clearly.

11. Let them digest. (Internal questioning takes place.)

12. Differing opinion forms (if it makes sense to them).

13. Change!

There are two possible outcomes.

One is that no change takes place based on stubbornness and saving face, though subconsciously they will think often about what was discussed, and change in the near future may be evident.

The other is they allow their minds to wander and consider there may be other options, ideas or thoughts that challenge what they have felt strongly about moments earlier. The latter is the quickest way to achieve change.

Remember, wisdom comes from different perspectives.

UNDERSTANDING THE UNCONSCIOUS MIND

The unconscious mind is always listening. The conscious mind is not.

The unconscious mind is what has the internal dialogues within your mind. Think of a time when you couldn't sleep because of the various thoughts going through your head.

It is important to feed the subconscious mind as much positive as possible. If not, it can weigh you down without realizing it.

Self-awareness is very important. Be aware of how you communicate, and your audience will pay huge dividends in life since not everyone receives information the same. You must implement this knowledge to achieve the success you desire.

CHAPTER 12

Determining Who You Want to Be

"Knowing your audience determines your success."

- *Anonymous*

As with people, each asshole is different. This book says these characteristics provide general guidelines in how to approach personality types and situations. Now is when you determine your approach to the type you want to be.

Are you someone who wants to trust everyone?

You live a much happier life. You don't have to look over your shoulder or be disappointed at every turn by those who let you down. Everyone is on your team and is protecting your best interests and likes you. You are also likely to be defended by those who like you and value you if someone is attempting to cross you.

The potential drawbacks are it is highly unlikely everyone is deserving of your trust. Letdown, betrayal and issues are sure to follow. You are leaving yourself exposed and with near certainty will be let down or crossed by someone.

Are you someone who wants to have a trusted team?

The team will defend you, give you the benefit of the doubt, offer support when you are likely to need it most and won't betray you for their own self-interest.

The potential drawback with a trusted team is you are, in fact, placing trust in one, two or many that may not be deserving of your trust. They could very well be playing you for their own gain. They can out you for wrongdoing or to simply further their career to bosses, competitors, clients or co-workers. This could lead to the ultimate downfall — loss of everything.

Are you someone who feels better trusting no one?

The benefits are not exposing yourself to betrayal with a false sense of trust and depending on others psychologically.

The potential drawbacks are a lack of support should anything pressing arise. It may be a power struggle within the company, for which you would like their support or an opportunity for them to throw you under the bus or to advance others, including themselves at your expense.

Your hope for being this type of asshole is that your results have benefited everyone enough where they feel they are better with you. Loyalty is thrown out the window for someone who trusts no one. The only thing that matters to them is what have you done for me lately. If you aren't benefiting them recently, the past benefits may be forgotten, and someone who is more beneficial to them and what they want will replace you.

Your Life, Your Decision

Ultimately, you must determine which route you can operate most effectively. One should always perform little tests of trust, such as gossip, trusted information only revealed to one source to see if it is spread. In doing so, you can establish whether trust is warranted. Assholes are needed in life, like it or not.

About the Author

Michael Anthony is the founder of The Institute of Human Understanding and is known for his research in the understanding of human interaction and reaction. He founded the Institute of Human Understanding on the belief that human decision-making can be predicted once the person's classification is identified and understood.

The Institute of Human Understanding has conducted more than 10 years of research and development to date, which includes understanding the psychology behind different personality types, how to communicate effectively verbally and non-verbally, as well as interpreting body language. It has also identified how to create a presence (the "it" factor).

Additionally, Mr. Anthony has traveled extensively throughout the United States and abroad. He has worked with people from more than 30 countries, including the United States, Canada, Sweden, India, Australia, Saudi Arabia, Egypt, Jordan, Germany, the Netherlands, Costa Rica, Italy, Spain, France, South Africa, Russia, England, Pakistan, Mexico, Israel, Syria, Malaysia, Lebanon, Turkey, North Korea, Slovakia, Finland, Thailand, Brazil, Japan, Puerto Rico, China and Singapore.

He is certified as a "Neuro-Linguistic Programmer" after having completed intense training in the field of Neuro-Linguistic Programming. Neuro-Linguistic Programming details from a linguists' and physicists' perspective how people think and make decisions. Mr. Anthony has also been certified as a "Master Practitioner" of Neuro-Linguistic Programming, after having completed further training and is also certified as a Master Practitioner in effectiveness and practice in his field.

Our goal is to improve the lives of others through human understanding.

The Institute of Human Understanding

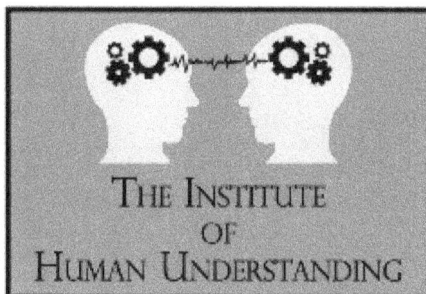

Principles for Success

- Strive to be happy, not content.

- Do not ever settle; the things you accept become the things you regret.

- Timing is everything.

- Be aware of how you think so you avoid falling into past failures.

- Knowledge without implementation is worse than implementation without knowledge.

www.TheInstituteOfHumanUnderstanding.com